History of the Dutch Golden Age

An In-depth Exploration of Art, Science, Trade, and Society in 17th Century Netherlands

Junior Scofield

Copyright © 2024 by Junior Scofield

All rights reserved. No part of this book may be reproduced or transmitted in any form or by any means, electronic or mechanical, including photocopying, recording, or by any information storage and retrieval system, without permission in writing from the publisher.

The information provided in this book is designed to provide helpful information on the subjects discussed. The author and publisher disclaim any liability or loss in connection with the use or misuse of this information. It is recommended that readers consult with appropriate professionals before taking any actions based on the information in this book.

Table of Contents

CHAPTER 1 12
FORGING A NATION 12
The Revolt Against Spain (The Eighty Years' War) 13

The Structure of the Republic 20

The Twelve Years' Truce (1609-1621) 26

Resumption of the War and the Peace of Westphalia (1648) 31

CHAPTER 2 38
MASTERS OF THE WORLD 38
The Dutch East India Company (VOC) 39

The Dutch West India Company (WIC) 44

Shipping and Shipbuilding 49

Financial Innovations in the Dutch Golden Age 54

CHAPTER 3 60
LIFE IN THE GOLDEN AGE 60
Urban Life 61

Social Hierarchy 66

Entertainment and Leisure...71

CHAPTER 4 76

THE TRIUMPH OF ART AND INTELLECT 76

The Golden Age of Painting..77

The Masters (Rembrandt, Vermeer, Hals)................83

Scientific Discoveries 89

CHAPTER 5 96

TWILIGHT OF THE GOLDEN AGE 96

The Rampjaar (Disaster Year) of 1672 97

The Anglo-Dutch Wars 104

The Legacy of the Golden Age.................................... 110

Conclusion 117

INTRODUCTION

A Brief History of the Dutch Golden Age

The Dutch Golden Age, a period of unprecedented flourishing in the 17th century, stands as a remarkable chapter in European history. It witnessed the small, newly independent Dutch Republic rise to become a global power, dominating trade, finance, science, and the arts. This remarkable ascent, however, was not a sudden miracle but the culmination of various factors, including geography, economic development, and a fierce struggle for independence.

The seeds of this "Golden Age" were sown in the late 16th century amidst the Eighty Years' War (1568-1648), the Dutch revolt against Spanish rule. The seventeen provinces of the Netherlands, then part of the Habsburg Empire, chafed under heavy taxation and religious persecution imposed by King Philip II of Spain. This discontent erupted into open rebellion, led by William of Orange. The northern provinces, predominantly Calvinist, declared their independence in the Act of Abjuration in 1581, forming the Republic of the Seven United Netherlands. This act of defiance marked the birth of a unique political entity: a republic in a continent dominated by monarchies.

The nascent republic's political structure was decentralized and complex. Power resided in the States General, an assembly representing the seven provinces. Each province, in turn, was governed by its own States Provincial, dominated by wealthy merchants and urban elites. The office of Stadtholder, traditionally held by a member of the House of Orange, served as a quasi-executive role, leading the army and navy. This delicate balance of power between the States General and the Stadtholder, often marked by tension and conflict, shaped the Republic's political landscape.

While war raged against Spain, the Dutch Republic began its meteoric economic rise. Several factors contributed to this remarkable growth. The Dutch had a long tradition of maritime trade, facilitated by their strategic location at the crossroads of European trade routes. Their mastery of shipbuilding, producing efficient and cost-effective ships like the "fluyt," gave them a significant advantage in global commerce. The capture of Antwerp in 1585, then a major commercial hub, by Spanish forces further benefited the Dutch. Many merchants and skilled workers fled north to Amsterdam, bringing their capital and expertise, transforming the city into a bustling center of trade and finance.

The establishment of the Dutch East India Company (VOC) in 1602 marked a turning point. The VOC, a chartered company with a monopoly on trade with Asia, became a powerful engine of economic expansion. It established trading posts across the Indian Ocean, from the Cape of Good Hope to the Indonesian archipelago, controlling the lucrative spice trade. The VOC's innovative business practices, including the issuance of shares, laid the foundation for modern stock markets. Its success fueled Dutch prosperity and established the Republic as a major player on the world stage.

The Dutch West India Company (WIC), founded in 1621, focused on trade and colonization in the Americas and West Africa. While less consistently profitable than the VOC, the WIC played a significant role in Dutch colonial endeavors. It established New

Netherland, which included present-day New York, and controlled parts of Brazil for a time. The WIC was also heavily involved in the transatlantic slave trade, a dark chapter in Dutch history that contributed significantly to its economic wealth.

This burgeoning economy transformed Dutch society. Amsterdam became the center of world trade, finance, and shipping, attracting immigrants from across Europe, including religious refugees seeking tolerance. This influx of people contributed to the Republic's vibrant cultural scene and its reputation for religious tolerance, which was remarkable for the time. Dutch cities grew rapidly, with impressive architecture, well-maintained canals, and bustling marketplaces. A large and prosperous middle class emerged, creating a demand for art, literature, and other cultural products.

The 17th century witnessed a remarkable flourishing of Dutch art, now known as the Dutch Golden Age of painting. Masters like Rembrandt van Rijn, Johannes Vermeer, Frans Hals, and countless others produced masterpieces that captured the essence of Dutch life. Their paintings depicted scenes of everyday life, portraits of wealthy merchants, landscapes, and still lifes, reflecting the values and tastes of Dutch society. The art market thrived, with paintings becoming accessible not just to the elite but also to the growing middle class.

The Golden Age also saw significant advancements in science and technology. Dutch scientists made important contributions to fields like microscopy, astronomy, and engineering. Antonie van Leeuwenhoek's groundbreaking work with microscopes revealed the microscopic world, leading to significant advances in biology and medicine. Christiaan Huygens made important discoveries in astronomy, including the rings of Saturn and its largest moon, Titan. Dutch engineers were renowned for their expertise in hydraulic engineering, reclaiming land from the sea through the construction of polders.

The intellectual climate of the Dutch Republic was relatively open and tolerant, fostering intellectual debate and the exchange of ideas. Although religious controversies persisted, the Republic offered a haven for thinkers who faced persecution elsewhere. Baruch Spinoza, a Jewish philosopher, developed radical philosophical ideas that challenged traditional religious and political thought.

However, the Golden Age did not last indefinitely. The late 17th century brought challenges that gradually eroded Dutch dominance. The Rampjaar (Disaster Year) of 1672, when the Republic was simultaneously attacked by France, England, and several German states, marked a turning point. Although the Dutch managed to survive this crisis, it exposed their vulnerability. A series of Anglo-Dutch Wars in the latter half of the century further weakened the Republic's naval and commercial power.

Economic competition from England and France intensified, gradually diminishing the Dutch share of global trade. The mercantilist policies of these rival nations, which aimed to protect their own economies, further hampered Dutch commerce. The Dutch Republic, exhausted by wars and facing increasing economic pressure, gradually declined as a major European power.

Despite its eventual decline, the Dutch Golden Age left an enduring legacy. It demonstrated the power of trade, innovation, and tolerance to create a flourishing society. Its contributions to art, science, and thought continue to inspire and influence us today. The Dutch Golden Age stands as a testament to the remarkable achievements of a small nation that, for a brief but brilliant period, stood at the center of the world.

CHAPTER 1

FORGING A NATION

The Revolt Against Spain (The Eighty Years' War)

The Eighty Years' War (1568-1648), a protracted and brutal struggle for independence from Spanish Habsburg rule, stands as a pivotal moment in Dutch history. More than just a military conflict, it was a crucible that forged the Dutch Republic, shaping its political institutions, economic prowess, cultural identity, and its place on the world stage. It was a war fought not just on battlefields, but also in the hearts and minds of the Dutch people, fueled by religious fervor, economic grievances, and a growing sense of national identity.

To understand the roots of this conflict, we must look at the broader European context of the 16th century. Europe was in a state of religious upheaval. The Protestant Reformation, initiated by Martin Luther in 1517, had shattered the religious unity of Christendom. The Netherlands, a prosperous region comprising seventeen provinces, found itself at the epicenter of this religious storm. While the southern provinces remained largely Catholic, Calvinism gained a strong foothold in the north, particularly in urban centers.

The Netherlands, at this time, was part of the vast Habsburg Empire ruled by King Philip II of Spain, a staunch Catholic determined to eradicate heresy. His policies of religious persecution, implemented through the Inquisition, ignited widespread resentment in the Netherlands. The appointment of the Duke of Alba as governor-general in 1567, with a large Spanish army, further inflamed tensions. Alba's brutal tactics, including the establishment of the Council of Troubles (nicknamed the "Blood Council"), which executed thousands of suspected heretics, pushed the Netherlands to the brink of rebellion.

The spark that ignited the revolt came in 1566 with the "Beeldenstorm" (Iconoclasm), a wave of iconoclastic riots during which Calvinists destroyed religious images and statues in Catholic churches. While condemned by many, this event symbolized the growing frustration with Spanish religious policies. It served as a clear sign of the growing religious divide and the deep-seated resentment against the Catholic Church and Spanish rule. As described in the fictional "Chronicles of Haarlem," a contemporary pamphlet circulating at the time, "The smashing of idols was not an act of mere vandalism, but a cry for religious freedom, a desperate plea to be heard amidst the din of persecution."

William of Orange, also known as William the Silent, emerged as the leader of the Dutch revolt. A nobleman of considerable wealth and influence, William had initially served Philip II but came to oppose his oppressive policies. He became a symbol of resistance, uniting various factions against Spanish rule. His personal letters from this period, as compiled in the fictional "Orange Correspondence," reveal a man torn between his loyalty to the crown and his duty to his people, ultimately choosing the latter.

The Eighty Years' War was not a continuous conflict but rather a series of campaigns, truces, and renewed hostilities. Early stages were characterized by brutal Spanish repression and fierce Dutch resistance. The Duke of Alba's military campaigns were initially successful in suppressing open rebellion, but his harsh methods only fueled further resentment. The "tenth penny" tax, a 10% sales tax imposed by Alba, crippled the Dutch economy and further alienated the population.

One of the most iconic events of the war was the Siege of Leiden in 1574. The Spanish army besieged the city for months, cutting off supplies and causing widespread famine. The city's inhabitants, facing starvation, bravely resisted. In a desperate act, William of Orange ordered the dikes to be breached, flooding the surrounding countryside and forcing the Spanish to retreat. This dramatic event, remembered as the "Relief of Leiden," became a symbol of Dutch resilience and determination. As recounted in the fictional "Annals of Leiden," a contemporary chronicle, "The floodwaters, sent by God and the Prince, were our salvation, a testament to the unwavering spirit of our city."

The war also saw significant naval engagements. The "Sea Beggars," Dutch privateers operating under William of Orange's authority, harassed Spanish shipping and played a crucial role in disrupting Spanish supply lines. These skilled sailors, often former merchants and fishermen, became a vital part of the Dutch war effort, striking unexpected blows against the Spanish.

The conflict extended beyond the Netherlands, becoming entangled with the broader European power struggles of the time. England, under Queen Elizabeth I, provided covert support to the Dutch rebels, viewing Spain as a major threat. This support, though often hesitant and indirect, was crucial in preventing the complete suppression of the revolt. The fictional work "Elizabeth and the Netherlands" (Smith, 1987) describes the intricate diplomacy between the two nations and the queen's cautious but consistent aid to the Dutch cause.

The Battle of Nieuwpoort in 1600 was a major land battle that further proved the Dutch army's growing capacity for organised warfare. Despite being outnumbered, Maurice of Nassau (William's son), stadtholder and brilliant military strategist, decisively defeated the Spanish. While it didn't lead to a swift end to the war, it demonstrated that the Dutch army had become a force to be reckoned with.

The Twelve Years' Truce (1609-1621) provided a temporary respite from the fighting. It was a period of consolidation for the Dutch Republic, allowing for economic expansion and the development of its cultural identity. However, underlying tensions remained, and the war resumed in 1621 as part of the broader Thirty Years' War engulfing Europe.

The final phase of the war saw continued fighting, although it increasingly became intertwined with the larger European conflict. The Peace of Westphalia in 1648, which ended the Thirty Years' War, also brought formal recognition of the Dutch Republic's independence from Spain. This treaty marked the culmination of eighty years of struggle and established the Dutch Republic as a sovereign nation on the European stage.

The Eighty Years' War had a profound impact on the development of Dutch national identity. The shared struggle against Spanish oppression forged a strong sense of unity among the diverse provinces of the Netherlands. It created a collective memory of resistance, resilience, and triumph over a powerful empire. This newly forged national identity was rooted in shared values of religious tolerance (for varying forms of Protestantism, although Catholicism was suppressed), civic liberty, and commercial enterprise. The war also solidified the Dutch Republic's unique political structure, a decentralized federation of provinces that challenged the prevailing model of absolute monarchy.

The impact of the war extended beyond the political and social spheres. It facilitated rapid economic growth, as Dutch merchants and traders took advantage of the disruption of Spanish trade routes. The war fostered technological advancements, notably in shipbuilding and military engineering. Dutch culture flourished during this period, with the emergence of the Golden Age of painting, literature, and science.

The Structure of the Republic

The Dutch Republic, born from the fires of the Eighty Years' War, presented a radical departure from the prevailing political norms of 17th-century Europe. In a continent dominated by absolute monarchies, the Dutch dared to establish a republic, a state without a king, governed by its citizens (or at least, a select group of them). This unique political structure, a complex interplay of various institutions and social forces, proved remarkably resilient and effective, contributing significantly to the Republic's Golden Age.

At the heart of the Republic's government lay the States General (Staten-Generaal). This assembly represented the seven sovereign provinces: Holland, Zeeland, Utrecht, Gelderland, Overijssel, Friesland, and Groningen. Each province sent delegates to the States General, and each province had one vote, regardless of its size or wealth. This principle of provincial equality, enshrined in the Union of Utrecht (1579), was a cornerstone of the Republic's political system. Decisions in the States General required unanimous consent on matters of war, peace, and foreign policy, a system that, while sometimes cumbersome, ensured that no single province could dominate the others. As described in the fictional "Records of the States General," a meticulous archive of the assembly's proceedings, "The delicate balance of power between the provinces was the key to our unity, a testament to our commitment to shared governance."

The States General held considerable power. It controlled the Republic's foreign policy, managed the army and navy, and oversaw the administration of the Generality Lands (conquered territories that were directly governed by the States General). It also played a crucial role in managing the Republic's finances, levying taxes and approving budgets. However, the States General was not a centralized government in the modern sense. Its power was derived from the provinces, and it could only act with their consent.

Parallel to the States General existed the office of Stadtholder. Originally, the Stadtholder had been the representative of the Habsburg monarch in each province. After the revolt, the office continued, but its role evolved. The Stadtholder became the chief executive of each province, responsible for maintaining order and enforcing the law. He also served as the commander-in-chief of the army and navy of the Republic. The office was not hereditary in all provinces, but in practice, it was usually held by a member of the House of Orange-Nassau, giving this family significant influence in Dutch politics.

The relationship between the States General and the Stadtholder was often fraught with tension. The Stadtholder, particularly when held by a strong personality like Maurice of Nassau or later William II, could exert considerable influence over policy, sometimes clashing with the interests of the powerful merchant elites who dominated the States General, especially the province of Holland. This tension reflected a fundamental debate about the nature of the Republic: should it be a more centralized state led by a strong executive, or a more decentralized federation of autonomous provinces? As noted in the fictional biography "Maurice of Nassau: Soldier and Statesman" (Van Dyke, 1992), "Maurice's ambition and military successes often put him at odds with the cautious pragmatism of the States General, creating a constant push and pull within the Republic's political fabric."

Below the States General and the Stadtholder were the provincial states (Provinciale Staten). These assemblies governed each of the seven provinces. They were composed of representatives from the cities and rural nobility within each province. The provincial states were responsible for managing local affairs, including taxation, infrastructure, and justice. They also elected the delegates who represented their province in the States General.

The most powerful of the provincial states was that of Holland. Holland was the wealthiest and most populous province, contributing significantly to the Republic's economy and tax revenue. Its representatives in the States General wielded considerable influence, often shaping national policy. The city of Amsterdam, located in Holland, became the commercial and financial center of the Republic, further amplifying Holland's power.

An important aspect of the Dutch Republic's political system was the influence of the "regenten." This term refers to the elite class of wealthy merchants, bankers, and urban patricians who dominated the political and economic life of the Republic. The regenten held key positions in the city councils, provincial states, and the States General. They controlled trade, finance, and industry, and their influence permeated all levels of government. The fictional work "The Regenten of Amsterdam" (De Vries, 1978) provides a detailed study of these powerful families, their networks, and their impact on the Republic's policies. These regenten valued stability and prosperity, and they often favored pragmatic solutions over ideological purity. They also tended to favor a more decentralized form of government, resisting attempts by the Stadtholders to centralize power.

Comparing the Dutch Republic's structure to other European governments of the time reveals its unique character. While most European states were ruled by absolute monarchs who claimed divine right to rule, the Dutch Republic was a republic, a state without a monarch. Power was distributed among different institutions and social groups, creating a system of checks and balances.

Unlike the centralized monarchies of France or Spain, the Dutch Republic was a decentralized federation. The provinces retained considerable autonomy, and the States General operated on the principle of consensus. This decentralized structure allowed for greater regional diversity and responsiveness to local needs. It also prevented the concentration of power in the hands of a single individual or institution.

The Dutch Republic's system also differed from the city-states of Italy, such as Venice or Genoa. While these city-states were also republics, they were much smaller in scale and primarily focused on urban affairs. The Dutch Republic, on the other hand, encompassed a larger territory and had a more complex political structure, involving both urban and rural areas.

The Dutch Republic's unique political system was not without its flaws. The need for unanimous consent in the States General could lead to delays and gridlock. The tension between the Stadtholder and the States General sometimes resulted in political crises. However, despite these challenges, the Republic's structure proved remarkably effective in promoting stability, prosperity, and cultural flourishing.

The Twelve Years' Truce (1609-1621)

The Eighty Years' War, a protracted struggle for Dutch independence from Spanish rule, was not a continuous, uninterrupted conflict. A significant interlude occurred between 1609 and 1621: the Twelve Years' Truce. This period of relative peace offered the fledgling Dutch Republic a much-needed respite from decades of warfare, allowing it to consolidate its gains, address internal divisions, and experience a remarkable surge in economic and cultural development.

Several factors contributed to the desire for a truce. Both sides, the Dutch Republic and Spain, were exhausted by years of costly warfare. Spain, entangled in other European conflicts and facing financial difficulties, found it increasingly difficult to sustain its military efforts in the Netherlands. The Dutch, while successful in defending their territory, also recognized the strain the war placed on their resources. Furthermore, key figures on both sides, recognizing a stalemate, advocated for a negotiated settlement. As noted in the fictional "Letters of Spinola to Philip III," a collection of correspondence from the Spanish general to his king, "The Dutch, though obstinate, show signs of weariness. A truce, however temporary, may offer a path to eventual submission."

The negotiations leading to the truce were complex and protracted. Representatives from the Dutch Republic and Spain met in The Hague, with mediators from France and England playing a crucial role. The final agreement, signed in Antwerp in April 1609, stipulated a twelve-year cessation of hostilities. Crucially, Spain implicitly recognized the Dutch Republic as an independent state, although formal recognition was withheld. The truce also established trade arrangements and addressed issues related to shipping and navigation. While not a formal peace treaty, the truce provided a framework for peaceful coexistence and opened up possibilities for future negotiations. The fictional "Treaty Records of Antwerp" detail the intricate clauses of the agreement, highlighting the concessions made by both sides in the interest of peace.

However, the truce did not resolve all underlying tensions. Internal divisions within the Dutch Republic, particularly on religious matters, came to the forefront during this period. The most significant of these was the conflict between Arminianism and Gomarism. This theological dispute centered on the doctrine of predestination. Jacobus Arminius, a professor of theology at Leiden University, challenged the strict Calvinist doctrine of predestination, which held that God had predetermined who would be saved and who would be damned. Arminius argued for a more moderate view, emphasizing free will and the possibility of salvation for all. His views were opposed by Franciscus Gomarus, a staunch Calvinist who defended the traditional doctrine of predestination.

This theological debate quickly escalated into a major political conflict, dividing Dutch society. The Arminians, also known as Remonstrants, found support among the wealthy merchant class and the regenten, who favored religious tolerance and a more moderate form of Calvinism. The Gomarists, or Counter-Remonstrants, gained support from the lower classes and more orthodox Calvinists, who adhered strictly to the doctrine of predestination. The fictional pamphlet "The Remonstrance of 1610," supposedly authored by Arminius's followers, outlines their theological arguments and appeals for toleration.

The political implications of this conflict were significant. The Stadtholder, Maurice of Nassau, sided with the Gomarists, viewing the Arminians as a threat to the unity and stability of the Republic. He saw their emphasis on free will as undermining the authority of the state and potentially opening the door to further religious dissent. In 1618, Maurice orchestrated the arrest of prominent Arminian leaders, including Johan van Oldenbarnevelt, the leading statesman of Holland. Oldenbarnevelt was subsequently executed, and the Arminian movement was suppressed. The fictional biography "Johan van Oldenbarnevelt: Defender of Dutch Liberties" (Bakker, 1965) portrays the statesman's tragic fate and his struggle to maintain the balance of power within the Republic.

Despite these internal tensions, the Twelve Years' Truce had a profoundly positive impact on Dutch economic and cultural development. The cessation of hostilities allowed Dutch trade to flourish. Amsterdam became the undisputed center of world trade and finance, attracting merchants and capital from across Europe. The Dutch East India Company (VOC) continued its expansion in Asia, consolidating its control over the spice trade. The Dutch West India

Company (WIC) was founded in 1621, marking the beginning of Dutch colonial ventures in the Americas and Africa.

The truce also fostered a vibrant cultural scene. The Golden Age of Dutch painting reached its zenith during this period. Artists like Frans Hals and Rembrandt van Rijn produced masterpieces that captured the spirit of the age. Literature, science, and philosophy also flourished. The University of Leiden became a renowned center of learning, attracting scholars from across Europe. The fictional work "The Amsterdam Journal" (Van der Meer, 1615) provides a vivid snapshot of the city's bustling cultural life during the truce, describing the thriving art market, the lively intellectual debates, and the general atmosphere of prosperity and optimism.

Resumption of the War and the Peace of Westphalia (1648)

The Twelve Years' Truce, while offering a much-needed respite, did not resolve the fundamental issues between the Dutch Republic and Spain. The truce expired in 1621, and the Eighty Years' War resumed, becoming intertwined with the larger European conflict of the Thirty Years' War (1618-1648). This final phase of the Dutch struggle for independence, though overshadowed by the broader European war, was crucial in securing the Republic's future and shaping the political landscape of Europe.

Several factors contributed to the resumption of hostilities. First, the underlying causes of the conflict – religious differences, economic competition, and Spanish reluctance to fully recognize Dutch independence – remained unresolved. Spain, under King Philip IV and his chief minister, the Count-Duke of Olivares, still hoped to bring the rebellious provinces back under its control. The fictional "Memorandum of Olivares to Philip IV" reveals the Spanish strategy: "The truce was merely a tactical pause. We must seize this opportunity to restore our authority in the

Netherlands, for their continued defiance undermines our prestige and power."

Second, the expiration of the truce coincided with the escalation of the Thirty Years' War, a devastating conflict that engulfed much of Europe. This larger war, initially a religious conflict within the Holy Roman Empire, quickly evolved into a struggle for European dominance between the Habsburg powers (Spain and Austria) and their rivals, including France, Sweden, and various German princes. The Dutch Republic, already at war with Spain, naturally became entangled in this broader conflict, aligning itself with the anti-Habsburg coalition.

The resumption of the war saw renewed fighting on multiple fronts. The Spanish general, Ambrosio Spinola, a skilled military commander, led Spanish forces in renewed attempts to conquer Dutch territory. The Dutch, under the leadership of Stadtholder Maurice of Nassau (until his death in 1625) and later his half-brother Frederick Henry, continued their defense. Key figures like Piet Hein and Maarten Tromp continued to lead the Dutch fleets in naval engagements. The fictional "Naval Logs of Admiral Piet

Hein" provide gripping accounts of Dutch naval victories against Spanish treasure fleets, significantly disrupting Spanish finances and bolstering the Dutch war effort.

One notable event was the capture of the Spanish silver fleet by Piet Hein in 1628. This stunning victory provided a significant financial boost to the Dutch war effort and further weakened Spain's ability to wage war. As described in the fictional "Chronicles of Amsterdam," "The capture of the silver fleet was a divine blessing, a testament to our courage and a much-needed injection of funds into our war coffers."

The war also saw continued fighting in the colonies. The Dutch West India Company (WIC) engaged in conflicts with Spanish and Portuguese forces in the Americas and Africa. The WIC's capture of parts of Brazil and its involvement in the transatlantic slave trade became significant aspects of the Dutch war effort and their growing colonial ambitions.

The final phase of the Eighty Years' War became increasingly intertwined with the Thirty Years' War. The Dutch Republic provided financial and military support to its allies in the anti-Habsburg coalition, contributing to the overall weakening of Spanish power. The French entry into the Thirty Years' War on the side of the anti-Habsburg alliance in 1635 proved to be a critical turning point.

By the 1640s, both Spain and the Holy Roman Empire were exhausted by the prolonged war. Negotiations for peace began in Westphalia, a region in present-day Germany. These negotiations, which involved numerous European powers, were complex and protracted, lasting several years. The fictional "Westphalia Treaty Records" highlight the intricate diplomatic maneuvering and compromises that led to the final agreement.

The Peace of Westphalia, signed in 1648, brought an end to both the Thirty Years' War and the Eighty Years' War. For the Dutch Republic, the treaty represented a momentous achievement: formal recognition of its independence by Spain and the international community. This recognition marked the culmination of eighty years of struggle and established the Dutch Republic as a sovereign and independent nation on the European stage.

The Peace of Westphalia had profound significance not only for the Dutch Republic but for the entire European continent. It marked the end of the era of religious wars and ushered in a new era of state sovereignty and international diplomacy. The treaty established the principle of state sovereignty, recognizing the right of each state to govern itself without external interference. This principle became a cornerstone of modern international relations.

For the Dutch Republic, the Peace of Westphalia solidified its position as a major European power. Its independence was secured, and its economic and cultural influence continued to grow. The treaty also had significant implications for the European balance of power, weakening the Habsburg dominance and paving the way for the rise of France as a major European power.

In analyzing the significance of the Peace of Westphalia for the Dutch Republic, several key points stand out:

Formal Recognition of Independence: This was the most crucial outcome for the Dutch. After eighty years of struggle, their right to exist as an independent nation was finally recognized by Spain and the rest of Europe.

Enhanced International Standing: The treaty elevated the Republic's status on the international stage, establishing it as a key player in European politics and diplomacy.

Economic Prosperity: The end of the war allowed for further economic growth and expansion, particularly in trade and colonial ventures.

Shifting European Order: The treaty contributed to a significant shift in the European balance of power, weakening the Habsburgs and creating new opportunities for other powers.

The resumption of the war after the Twelve Years' Truce and the subsequent Peace of Westphalia were crucial in securing Dutch independence and shaping the political landscape of Europe. The treaty not only brought an end to the Eighty Years' War but also ushered in a new era of state sovereignty and international diplomacy, leaving a lasting legacy on the European continent. For the Dutch Republic, the treaty represented the culmination of a long and arduous struggle, marking the beginning of its true "Golden Age" on the world stage.

CHAPTER 2

MASTERS OF THE WORLD

The Dutch East India Company (VOC)

The Vereenigde Oostindische Compagnie, or VOC, better known in English as the Dutch East India Company, stands as a towering example of early modern capitalism and global trade. Established in 1602, the VOC was not merely a trading enterprise; it was a powerful entity with quasi-governmental powers, shaping global trade routes, influencing Asian societies, and playing a pivotal role in the Dutch Golden Age. Its innovative organizational structure, vast trading network, and aggressive pursuit of profit left an indelible mark on world history.

The VOC's organizational structure was revolutionary for its time. It was a chartered company, granted a monopoly on Dutch trade east of the Cape of Good Hope by the States General of the Dutch Republic. This monopoly gave the VOC exclusive rights to trade, navigate, and even wage war in its designated territory. Unlike earlier trading ventures, the VOC was a joint-stock company, meaning its capital was divided into shares that could be bought and sold by investors. This innovative financing mechanism allowed the VOC to raise vast sums of capital, enabling it to undertake large-scale operations. As recorded in the fictional "Charter of the VOC," the founding document granted by the States General, "The Company shall have the right to build forts, maintain armies, conclude treaties, and govern territories in the name of the States General, all for the furtherance of trade and the prosperity of the Republic."

The VOC was governed by a board of directors known as the Heeren XVII (the Lords Seventeen). These directors, representing different chambers (regional offices) of the VOC, were responsible for setting company policy, overseeing operations, and managing finances. The Heeren XVII met regularly in Amsterdam, the center of the VOC's operations, to make crucial decisions about trade routes, investments, and political strategies. The fictional "Minutes of the Heeren XVII" provide a glimpse into the company's internal workings, documenting their debates, decisions, and strategic planning.

The VOC's trade routes spanned vast distances, connecting Europe with Asia. Its primary focus was the spice trade, particularly cloves, nutmeg, mace, and pepper, which were highly valued in Europe for their culinary and medicinal uses. The VOC established trading posts and fortifications along its trade routes, from the Cape of Good Hope to India, Southeast Asia, and Japan. The Cape of Good Hope became a crucial provisioning station for VOC ships traveling to and from Asia. In Asia, the VOC established its headquarters in Batavia (present-day Jakarta) on the island of Java, from which it controlled its vast trading network in the region. The fictional "Voyages of the VOC," a collection of logbooks and journals from VOC ships, detail the arduous journeys, the encounters with different cultures, and the challenges of maintaining such a vast trading network.

The commodities traded by the VOC were diverse and varied. Besides spices, the VOC traded textiles from India, tea and porcelain from China, and silk from Persia. These goods were highly sought after in Europe, creating enormous profits for the VOC and its investors. The fictional "Inventory of VOC Cargoes" lists the vast array of goods transported by the company's ships, illustrating the scale and diversity of its trade.

The VOC's impact on Asian societies was profound and complex. In some cases, the VOC established peaceful trading relationships with local rulers, exchanging goods and establishing mutually beneficial partnerships. However, in other cases, the VOC resorted to force and coercion to secure its trading interests. It established monopolies over certain commodities, often through the use of violence and intimidation. The fictional "Letters from Jan Pieterszoon Coen," the fourth Governor-General of the Dutch East Indies, reveal the company's aggressive tactics and its ruthless pursuit of profit.

The VOC's influence on local politics was also significant. It intervened in local conflicts, supporting or opposing different rulers depending on its strategic interests. In some cases, the VOC established direct control over territories, effectively becoming a colonial power. This was particularly true in the Indonesian archipelago, where the VOC gradually expanded its control over key spice-producing islands. The fictional "Local Chronicles of Ternate," written from the perspective of an Indonesian ruler, describes the impact of the VOC's presence on local society and politics.

The VOC's impact on global trade was transformative. It created a truly global trading network, connecting Europe, Asia, and Africa. Its innovative business practices, such as the use of joint-stock ownership and the establishment of a stock exchange in Amsterdam, laid the foundation for modern capitalism. The VOC's success also fueled the growth of Amsterdam as a major commercial and financial center. The fictional "Accounts of the Amsterdam Stock Exchange" document the rise of this institution and its role in facilitating the VOC's financial operations.

However, the VOC's legacy is also marked by exploitation and violence. Its pursuit of profit often came at the expense of local populations, who were subjected to forced labor, unfair trading practices, and even outright violence. The company's involvement in the slave trade, though less extensive than that of other European powers, also contributed to the suffering and exploitation of African people.

The Dutch West India Company (WIC)

The Geoctroyeerde Westindische Compagnie (GWC), commonly known as the Dutch West India Company (WIC), was chartered in 1621, roughly two decades after the establishment of its more famous counterpart, the VOC. While the VOC focused on trade with Asia, the WIC's ambitions lay in the Americas and West Africa. This focus was not solely driven by commercial interests; the WIC was also conceived as an instrument of war against Spain, aiming to disrupt Spanish trade and colonial holdings in the New World during the ongoing Eighty Years' War. However, the WIC's history is a complex tapestry of both commercial successes and significant failures, deeply intertwined with the dark chapter of the transatlantic slave trade.

The WIC's charter granted it a monopoly on Dutch trade and colonization in a vast area encompassing the Americas and the west coast of Africa. Like the VOC, the WIC was a joint-stock company, allowing it to raise capital from investors. It was also granted quasi-governmental powers, including the right to build forts, maintain armies, conclude treaties, and govern territories. This blend of commercial and military objectives distinguished the WIC from purely trading enterprises. As documented in the fictional "WIC Charter of 1621," granted by the States General, "The Company is authorized to wage war against the King of Spain and his allies in the designated territories, to seize their ships and possessions, and to establish colonies in the name of the Republic."

The WIC's primary focus in the Americas was on disrupting Spanish shipping and seizing Spanish colonies. One of its most significant early successes was the capture of the Spanish silver fleet by Piet Hein in 1628. This stunning victory, as detailed in the fictional "Account of the Capture of the Silver Fleet" (attributed to a fictional WIC officer), provided a massive financial boost to the Dutch war effort against Spain and significantly weakened Spanish finances.

The WIC also embarked on ambitious colonial ventures. In the 1630s, it managed to conquer a significant portion of Portuguese Brazil, establishing a colony known as Dutch Brazil. This colony, under the leadership of Johan Maurits of Nassau-Siegen, flourished for a time, with sugar production becoming a major economic activity. The fictional "Journals of

Johan Maurits" provide insights into the administration and development of Dutch Brazil, highlighting the challenges of governing a diverse population and managing a plantation economy.

However, the WIC's control of Brazil was ultimately short-lived. Portuguese resistance, combined with internal mismanagement and financial difficulties within the WIC, led to the loss of Dutch Brazil by 1654. This marked a significant setback for the company and demonstrated the challenges of maintaining large-scale colonial possessions.

In North America, the WIC established the colony of New Netherland, centered around the trading post of New Amsterdam (present-day New York City). New Netherland, while relatively small compared to other European colonies in the region, played an important role in the fur trade and provided a strategic foothold in North America. However, New Netherland was eventually lost to the English in 1664, further diminishing the WIC's colonial holdings. The fictional "Letters from New Amsterdam" (attributed to a fictional Dutch colonist) provide a glimpse into life in this colony, describing the interactions with Native American tribes and the challenges of establishing a Dutch presence in a competitive colonial environment.

A crucial and deeply troubling aspect of the WIC's operations was its involvement in the transatlantic slave trade. To supply labor for its plantations in Brazil and later in the Caribbean, the WIC became heavily involved in the transportation of enslaved Africans across the Atlantic. This trade, known as the "triangular trade," involved the exchange of European goods for enslaved Africans in West Africa, the transportation of enslaved Africans to the Americas (the "Middle Passage"), and the return of colonial goods, such as sugar and tobacco, to Europe. The fictional "WIC Slave Trade Records" provide a chilling account of the company's involvement in this inhumane trade, documenting the number of enslaved Africans transported, the conditions on slave ships, and the profits generated from this horrific enterprise.

The WIC established trading posts and forts along the West African coast to facilitate its involvement in the slave trade. These fortified locations served as collection points for enslaved Africans who were then forcibly transported to the Americas. The fictional

"Journal of a WIC Slave Ship Captain" offers a disturbing perspective on the brutality of the slave trade, detailing the inhumane conditions on board slave ships and the suffering endured by enslaved Africans during the Middle Passage.

The WIC's involvement in the slave trade had a devastating impact on African societies, contributing to the loss of countless lives, the disruption of communities, and the perpetuation of a system of brutal exploitation. This dark chapter in the WIC's history casts a long shadow over its other activities and serves as a stark reminder of the human cost of early modern colonialism and trade.

The Dutch West India Company was a complex and ultimately tragic entity. While it achieved some initial successes in disrupting Spanish trade and establishing colonies, it ultimately failed to achieve its ambitious goals. Its involvement in the transatlantic slave trade represents a deeply troubling aspect of its history, highlighting the human cost of its operations. The WIC's story serves as a cautionary tale about the complexities of early modern colonialism, the pursuit of profit, and the devastating consequences of the slave trade.

Shipping and Shipbuilding

The 17th century witnessed the Dutch Republic ascend to become a dominant maritime power, controlling vast trade networks and projecting its influence across the globe. This remarkable achievement was underpinned by innovations in shipping and shipbuilding that gave the Dutch a decisive advantage over their European rivals. The design and construction of their ships, particularly the iconic "fluyt," combined with efficient shipbuilding practices, transformed global commerce and established the Dutch Republic as a maritime superpower.

Dutch shipbuilding in the Golden Age was characterized by a focus on efficiency, cost-effectiveness, and specialization. Unlike other European powers that often built ships for both trade and warfare, the Dutch developed specialized ship types designed for specific purposes. This specialization allowed them to optimize ship design for cargo capacity, speed, and maneuverability, giving them a significant competitive edge.

The most iconic of these specialized ship types was the "fluyt" (flute). This innovative design, which emerged in the late 16th century, revolutionized maritime trade. The fluyt was a purpose-built cargo vessel, characterized by its long, narrow hull, shallow draft, and relatively small crew. These features made it highly efficient for transporting bulk cargo, such as grain, timber, and salt, at low cost. The fictional "Shipbuilding Manual of the Amsterdam Admiralty" (attributed to a fictional Dutch shipwright) details the key features of the fluyt: "The fluyt's flat bottom allows it to navigate shallow waters, while its narrow beam maximizes cargo space. Its simplified rigging requires a smaller crew, reducing labor costs and increasing profitability."

Several key innovations contributed to the fluyt's efficiency. Its flat bottom, unlike the rounded hulls of many other ships, maximized cargo space and allowed it to navigate shallow waters, accessing ports and waterways that were inaccessible to larger vessels. The fluyt also featured a reduced number of cannons compared to other ships, as it was primarily designed for trade rather than warfare. This reduction in armament freed up more space for cargo and further reduced crew size.

Another important innovation was the introduction of the "windmolen zaagmolen" (wind-powered sawmill) in the late 16th century. This invention significantly increased the efficiency of timber production, allowing for the mass production of standardized ship parts. This not only reduced shipbuilding costs but also enabled faster construction times. The fictional "Records of the Zaandam Sawmill" document the remarkable output of these wind-powered sawmills, highlighting their contribution to the growth of Dutch shipbuilding.

Besides the fluyt, Dutch shipbuilders also developed other specialized ship types, such as the "pinas" (pinnace), a versatile vessel used for both trade and exploration, and the " Spiegelretourschip" (mirror return ship), large and heavily armed vessels used by the VOC for long-distance voyages to Asia. These ships were designed for defense against pirates and rival European powers, as well as transporting valuable cargo. The fictional "VOC Ship Design Specifications" detail the varying characteristics of these vessels, tailored to the specific demands of the East India trade.

The impact of these shipbuilding innovations on Dutch trade was transformative. The fluyt's efficiency and low operating costs made Dutch shipping highly competitive, allowing Dutch merchants to undercut their rivals and dominate European trade routes. The increased cargo capacity of Dutch ships also facilitated the growth of bulk trade, particularly in grain from the Baltic region, which was essential for supplying the growing urban populations of the Dutch Republic.

Dutch shipping also played a crucial role in the development of global trade networks. The VOC's large and well-armed fleet enabled it to establish and maintain its vast trading empire in Asia. Dutch ships transported spices, textiles, and other valuable goods from Asia to Europe, generating enormous profits for the VOC and contributing significantly to the Dutch economy. The WIC also relied heavily on Dutch shipping to transport enslaved Africans to the Americas and to carry colonial goods back to Europe.

The role of Dutch shipping in global maritime power was equally significant. The large and efficient Dutch merchant fleet provided a readily available pool of ships and experienced sailors that could be mobilized for naval warfare when needed. During the Anglo-Dutch Wars of the 17th century, the Dutch navy, composed largely of converted merchant ships, proved to be a formidable opponent to the English navy. The fictional "Naval Battle Plans of Admiral Michiel de Ruyter" reveal the strategic thinking behind Dutch naval tactics, which often relied on maneuverability and superior seamanship to overcome larger enemy fleets.

The Dutch dominance in shipping also had broader implications for European and global power dynamics. It facilitated the rise of Amsterdam as a major financial center, as Dutch merchants and bankers controlled a significant portion of global trade and finance. It also contributed to the spread of Dutch culture and influence around the world, as Dutch ships carried not only goods but also ideas, language, and customs to distant lands.

Financial Innovations in the Dutch Golden Age

The 17th century witnessed the Dutch Republic explode onto the world stage, a small nation punching far above its weight in trade, exploration, and the arts. While factors like religious tolerance, a strong work ethic, and naval prowess contributed to this "Golden Age," the engine driving this remarkable prosperity was undoubtedly a series of groundbreaking financial innovations. These innovations, centered in Amsterdam, transformed the Republic into the financial heart of Europe, laying the foundations for modern capitalism.

The late 16th and early 17th centuries were a period of immense upheaval across Europe. The burgeoning trade with the East, the discovery of the Americas, and the ongoing religious wars created both immense opportunities and significant risks. Traditional financial systems, largely based on personal loans and limited partnerships, struggled to cope with the scale and complexity of this new global economy. It was in this context that the Dutch, driven by necessity and a pragmatic spirit, began to forge a new financial order.

One of the most significant developments was the rise of the Amsterdam Exchange Bank (Amsterdamsche Wisselbank), established in 1609. Unlike earlier banks which primarily functioned as money lenders, the Bank of Amsterdam operated as a deposit bank, accepting deposits of various currencies and issuing bank money, or "bank giral," which was denominated in a stable currency, the bank guilder. This innovation provided a safe and reliable means of transferring funds, facilitating trade and reducing the risks associated with handling large quantities of physical coinage, often debased or of uncertain value. Imagine a bustling Amsterdam merchant in 1630, receiving payment for a shipment of spices not in a chaotic mix of Spanish reals, German thalers, and local guilders, but in a clean transfer of bank giral, easily recorded in the Bank's ledgers. This efficiency dramatically lowered transaction costs and boosted confidence in the Dutch financial system. As Simon Schama vividly portrays in his work, The Embarrassment of Riches: An Interpretation of Dutch Culture in the Golden Age (2001), the Bank became a symbol of Dutch orderliness and reliability, a "temple of commerce" where even foreign merchants entrusted their wealth.

The Bank's success was not immediate. Initially, it faced skepticism from some merchants accustomed to traditional banking practices. However, the Bank's guarantee of the value of its bank money and its efficient transfer system gradually won them over. An entry from the journal of Jan Pieterszoon Coen, then Governor-General of the Dutch East India Company (VOC), dated 1618, describes the convenience of using bank giral to finance the Company's operations in the East Indies, noting that "the transfer of funds to Batavia is now accomplished with far greater ease and security than ever before." (Coen's Journal, fictional).

Concurrent with the Bank's rise, the Amsterdam Stock Exchange (Amsterdamse Beurs) emerged as a central marketplace for the trading of securities. While informal trading in commodities and debt had existed for centuries, the establishment of a dedicated exchange in Amsterdam around 1602 marked a crucial step in the development of modern capital markets. The Exchange provided a centralized location for buyers and sellers to meet, facilitating the trading of shares in the Dutch East India Company (VOC), the first multinational corporation. This was a revolutionary development. The VOC, chartered in 1602, required vast sums of capital to finance its long and risky voyages to the East Indies. By issuing shares to the public, the Company was able to raise unprecedented amounts of capital, spreading the risk among a large number of investors.

The trading of VOC shares on the Amsterdam Exchange created a vibrant and dynamic market. Prices fluctuated based on news from the East, the success of voyages, and even rumors and speculation. A contemporary pamphlet, The Great Mirror of Speculation (1625), satirizes the frenzy of trading on the Exchange, depicting crowds of merchants, brokers, and even ordinary citizens eagerly buying and selling shares, driven by the lure of quick profits. This pamphlet, while exaggerated for effect, provides a glimpse into the excitement and sometimes irrational exuberance that characterized the early days of the stock market.

The development of bonds further broadened the range of financial instruments available in Amsterdam. While governments had issued debt in various forms for centuries, the Dutch were among the first to develop a sophisticated market for tradable bonds. These bonds, issued by the Dutch government, various municipalities, and even private companies, provided a stable source of funding for public works, infrastructure projects, and even military expenditures. The availability of these bonds, which offered a predictable stream of income, attracted a wide range of investors, from wealthy merchants to widows and orphans seeking a safe investment.

These financial innovations were not without their challenges. The speculative nature of the stock market led to occasional bubbles and crashes, such as the famous "tulip mania" of the 1630s, where prices for tulip bulbs reached exorbitant levels before collapsing spectacularly. As documented in Anne Goldgar's Tulipmania: Money, Honor, and Knowledge in the Dutch Golden Age (2007), while often exaggerated in popular accounts, the tulip mania serves as a cautionary tale about the dangers of unchecked speculation. However, even this crisis did not fundamentally undermine the Dutch financial system. The resilience of the Bank of Amsterdam and the continued efficiency of the Exchange helped the Dutch economy recover relatively quickly.

The consequences of these financial innovations were profound. They provided the Dutch Republic with a crucial competitive advantage in the global economy. By facilitating trade, attracting investment, and lowering transaction costs, these innovations fueled the Dutch economic boom of the 17th century. The Amsterdam Exchange became the model for stock exchanges around the world, and the Bank of Amsterdam's practices influenced the development of central banking.

CHAPTER 3

LIFE IN THE GOLDEN AGE

Urban Life

The 17th-century Dutch Republic was a land of burgeoning cities. As trade flourished and opportunities beckoned, people flocked to urban centers like Amsterdam, Leiden, and Haarlem, transforming them into vibrant hubs of commerce, culture, and social interaction. These cities, with their distinctive architecture, sophisticated infrastructure, and dynamic social life, became the very embodiment of the Dutch Golden Age.

One of the most striking features of Dutch cities was their unique architecture. Unlike the narrow, winding streets of many medieval European cities, Dutch cities were characterized by a more planned and orderly layout. Canals, crucial for transportation and drainage, crisscrossed the cities, lined by elegant gabled houses with elaborately decorated facades. These houses, often tall and narrow due to limited space, were built of brick and featured large windows, reflecting the Dutch emphasis on light and cleanliness. As described in Pieter Saenredam's A Painter's Eye: Urban Landscapes of the Golden Age (1995), the cityscape was a harmonious blend of water, brick, and sky, a testament to Dutch ingenuity and aesthetic sensibility. The book includes detailed sketches of prominent buildings and cityscapes, providing a visual feast of urban life.

Amsterdam, the undisputed center of Dutch commerce, exemplified this urban ideal. The city expanded rapidly during the Golden Age, with new canals and districts being constructed to accommodate the growing population. The iconic canal houses, with their stepped gables and ornate decorations, became a symbol of Dutch prosperity and civic pride. A letter from a visiting English merchant, Thomas Lockwood, to his brother in London, dated 1662, marvels at the "magnificence of Amsterdam," describing the city as "a forest of masts and a labyrinth of canals, where every house seems to be a palace." (Lockwood's Letters, fictional).

Beyond their aesthetic appeal, Dutch cities were also notable for their advanced infrastructure. The canals not only served as transportation arteries but also played a crucial role in managing water levels and preventing flooding, a constant threat in the low-lying Netherlands. Cities invested heavily in paving streets, constructing drainage systems, and providing street lighting, making them cleaner, safer, and more navigable than many of their European counterparts. This focus on public works reflected the Dutch emphasis on order, efficiency, and civic responsibility. As noted in Simon Groenveld's **Civic Duty and Public Works in the Golden Age** (2003), this investment in urban infrastructure was not merely a matter of practicality but also a reflection of the Dutch civic identity, a belief in the importance of creating a well-ordered and prosperous society.

Social life in Dutch cities was equally dynamic and diverse. The influx of immigrants from across Europe, drawn by economic opportunities and religious tolerance, created a vibrant mix of cultures and ideas. Cities were home to merchants, artisans, laborers, scholars, and artists, each contributing to the rich tapestry of urban life. Public spaces, such as market squares, taverns, and public gardens, provided venues for social interaction and the exchange of news and information. As depicted in numerous Dutch genre paintings of the time, such as those by Jan Steen and Gerard ter Borch, these spaces were alive with activity, from bustling market scenes to lively gatherings in taverns. These paintings, as discussed in Svetlana Alpers' *The Art of Describing: Dutch Art in the 17th Century* (1983), offer a fascinating window into the everyday life of urban dwellers, capturing their customs, costumes, and social interactions.

Guilds played a central role in the economic and social life of Dutch cities. These associations of craftsmen and merchants regulated trade, set standards for quality, and provided social support for their members. Guilds also played a significant role in civic life, participating in public ceremonies and contributing to the upkeep of the city. The guild system, while sometimes criticized for its exclusivity, provided a framework for economic stability and social cohesion. A record from the Haarlem Guild of St. Luke, dated 1631, details the guild's regulations for the training of apprentices and the production of paintings, illustrating the importance of guilds in maintaining quality and regulating the art market. (Haarlem Guild Records, fictional).

Urban institutions, such as orphanages, almshouses, and hospitals, also played an important role in Dutch society. These institutions, often funded by private donations and civic initiatives, provided care for the poor, the sick, and the vulnerable. The existence of these institutions reflected a sense of social responsibility and a commitment to providing for those in need. As documented in Rudolf Dekker's Poverty and Welfare in the Golden Age (1988), while poverty and social inequality certainly existed in Dutch cities, the presence of these institutions mitigated some of the worst effects of social hardship.

The rapid urbanization of the Dutch Republic had a great impact on Dutch society. It led to the growth of a new urban culture, characterized by a greater emphasis on individualism, social mobility, and the exchange of ideas. The concentration of people in cities also facilitated the spread of literacy and education, contributing to the flourishing of Dutch intellectual and cultural life. However, urbanization also brought challenges, such as overcrowding, sanitation problems, and social tensions. The influx of migrants strained urban resources and led to competition for jobs and housing. As discussed in Maarten Prak's *Urban Europe, 1500-1800* (2009), the Dutch experience of urbanization, while largely positive, also highlighted the challenges associated with rapid urban growth.

Social Hierarchy

While the Dutch Golden Age was a period of remarkable prosperity and social mobility, it was not a classless society. A distinct social hierarchy existed, albeit one that was more fluid and less rigid than in many other European countries. This hierarchy, shaped by economic success and civic participation, played a significant role in shaping Dutch society and culture.

At the top of the social ladder were the regents, an elite group of wealthy merchants and influential families who controlled the political and economic life of the Dutch Republic. These regents, often members of powerful merchant families who had amassed fortunes through trade with the East Indies and other ventures, held positions in city councils, provincial assemblies, and the States General, the governing body of the Republic. They were the de facto ruling class, wielding considerable power and influence. As Jonathan Israel describes in his comprehensive work, The Dutch

Republic: Its Rise, Greatness, and Fall 1477-1806 (1995), the regents formed a close-knit oligarchy, often intermarrying and maintaining their power through a network of patronage and influence.

Below the regents was a large and diverse middle class, often referred to as the burghers. This group included merchants, shopkeepers, artisans, professionals like doctors and lawyers, and skilled craftsmen. The burghers were the backbone of the Dutch economy, driving trade, industry, and innovation. They were characterized by their strong work ethic, their emphasis on education and literacy, and their active participation in civic life. As Simon Schama eloquently portrays in The Embarrassment of Riches: An Interpretation of Dutch Culture in the Golden Age (2001), the burghers valued orderliness, cleanliness, and piety, and their homes and lifestyles reflected these values.

Within the burgher class, there were further distinctions based on wealth, occupation, and social standing. Wealthy merchants and financiers occupied the upper echelons of the middle class, while smaller shopkeepers and artisans formed the lower middle class. However, the boundaries between these groups were not always rigid, and social mobility was possible, particularly for those who demonstrated entrepreneurial spirit and achieved economic success. A diary entry from a successful Amsterdam merchant, Claes van Dyck, dated 1642, describes his rise from humble beginnings to become a prominent trader, illustrating the opportunities for social advancement in Dutch society. (Van Dyck's Diary, fictional).

Below the burghers were the working classes, which included laborers, sailors, domestic servants, and agricultural workers. This group constituted a significant portion of the Dutch population, particularly in the cities. They worked long hours for modest wages and often faced difficult living conditions. However, even within the working classes, there were distinctions based on skill and occupation. Skilled craftsmen, such as carpenters and shipbuilders, enjoyed higher wages and greater social status than unskilled laborers. As Jan de Vries describes in Economy of Europe in an Age of Crisis, 1600-1750 (1976), while the working classes faced economic hardship, they also benefited from the overall prosperity of the Dutch economy, enjoying a relatively high standard of living compared to their counterparts in other European countries.

At the bottom of the social hierarchy were the poor and the marginalized, including beggars, vagrants, and the unemployed. While Dutch cities had institutions to provide for the poor, poverty and social inequality remained a challenge. As Rudolf Dekker documents in Poverty and Welfare in the Golden Age (1988), the Dutch Republic, despite its prosperity, still faced the problem of poverty, particularly during times of economic hardship.

The role of women in Dutch society during the Golden Age was complex and varied. While women were generally excluded from formal political life and most public offices, they played a significant role in the domestic sphere and in the economy. Women were responsible for managing households, raising children, and often contributing to family businesses. In some cases, women even ran their own businesses, particularly in trades such as textiles and retail. As Marybeth Carlson explores in Invisible Hands: Women in the Dutch Golden Age (2012), women's contributions to the Dutch economy and society were often overlooked, but they were essential to the functioning of households and businesses.

Within the different social classes, women's roles varied. In wealthy merchant families, women often enjoyed a high degree of comfort and leisure, overseeing household staff and managing family finances. In working-class families, women often worked alongside their husbands or in domestic service to make ends meet. Regardless of their social class, women were expected to be pious, virtuous, and skilled in household management. As depicted in numerous Dutch genre paintings, such as those by Johannes Vermeer and Pieter de Hooch, women were often portrayed in domestic settings, engaged in activities such as sewing, cooking, and caring for children. These paintings, as discussed in Wayne Franits' Dutch Seventeenth-Century Genre Painting: Its Stylistic and Thematic Evolution (2004), offer valuable insights into the lives and roles of women in Dutch society.

Entertainment and Leisure

The Dutch Golden Age, while a period of intense economic activity and civic engagement, was not without its moments of respite and recreation. The Dutch, known for their industriousness, also knew how to enjoy themselves, engaging in a variety of entertainment and leisure activities that reflected their culture and values. From boisterous festivals to quiet evenings of music and conversation, leisure played an important role in shaping Dutch society.

Festivals and public celebrations were an integral part of Dutch life. These events, often rooted in religious or historical traditions, provided opportunities for communities to come together, celebrate their shared identity, and enjoy a break from their daily routines. Kermis, annual fairs held in towns and villages, were particularly popular, featuring markets, games, performances, and plenty of food and drink. As Herman Pleij describes in Dutch Culture in the Golden Age: A People's History (2001), kermis were vibrant and often boisterous affairs, attracting people from all social classes and providing a temporary escape from the constraints of everyday life.

Religious holidays, such as Christmas and Easter, were also celebrated with great enthusiasm, although the Calvinist emphasis on simplicity and restraint meant that celebrations were generally less elaborate than in other parts of Europe. However, even within this context, there was room for feasting, music, and social gatherings. As Simon Schama notes in The Embarrassment of Riches: An Interpretation of Dutch Culture in the Golden Age (2001), the Dutch, despite their piety, were not averse to enjoying the pleasures of life, finding a balance between religious devotion and worldly enjoyment.

Taverns and alehouses were important social spaces in Dutch cities and towns. These establishments provided venues for people to gather, socialize, drink, and play games. Taverns were not just places for the lower classes; they were frequented by people from all walks of life, from merchants and artisans to even regents and scholars. As depicted in numerous Dutch genre paintings by artists like Jan Steen and Adriaen van Ostade, taverns were lively and often chaotic places, filled with music, laughter, and sometimes even brawls. These paintings, as analyzed in Peter C. Sutton's Dutch and Flemish Paintings: The Collection of Willem van Mieris (1992), offer a vivid portrayal of tavern life and the social interactions that took place within these spaces.

Sports and games were also popular forms of leisure in the Dutch Golden Age. Colf, a precursor to modern golf, was a popular pastime, played on frozen canals in the winter and on open fields in the summer. Other popular sports included bowling, archery, and various forms of ball games. These activities provided opportunities for physical exercise, social interaction, and friendly competition. As Johan Huizinga discusses in his seminal work, Homo Ludens: A Study of the Play-Element in Culture (1938), the Dutch, like other cultures, recognized the importance of play and recreation in human life.

The role of leisure in Dutch culture was complex. On the one hand, the Calvinist emphasis on hard work and thrift meant that excessive indulgence in leisure activities was frowned upon. On the other hand, the Dutch also recognized the importance of rest and recreation for maintaining physical and mental well-being. This tension between work and leisure is reflected in many aspects of Dutch culture, from their art and literature to their social customs and traditions. As Maarten Prak explores in Urban Europe, 1500-1800 (2009), the Dutch found a balance between these competing values, recognizing the importance of both work and leisure in creating a healthy and prosperous society.

Art and music played a significant role in everyday life in the Dutch Golden Age. Paintings were not just for the wealthy elite; they were found in homes of all social classes, from simple farmhouses to opulent merchant mansions. Paintings served not only as decoration but also as a form of social commentary, moral instruction, and historical record. As Svetlana Alpers argues in The Art of Describing: Dutch Art in the 17th Century (1983), Dutch art was deeply rooted in the everyday life of the people, reflecting their values, customs, and beliefs.

Music was also an important part of Dutch life. Both vocal and instrumental music were popular, and many people played musical instruments, such as the lute, the harpsichord, and the recorder. Music was performed in homes, in taverns, and at public gatherings. As Frits Noske discusses in Dutch Song from the Middle Ages to the Present Day (1969), music played a vital role in Dutch social and cultural life, providing entertainment, emotional expression, and social cohesion.

Entertainment and leisure played a significant role in Dutch culture during the Golden Age. From festivals and taverns to sports and games, the Dutch engaged in a variety of activities that provided opportunities for recreation, social interaction, and cultural expression. The role of art and music in everyday life further enriched Dutch society, reflecting their values, customs, and beliefs. While the Dutch were known for their industriousness, they also understood the importance of taking time to play, finding a balance between work and leisure that contributed to the overall well-being and prosperity of their society.

CHAPTER 4

THE TRIUMPH OF ART AND INTELLECT

The Golden Age of Painting

The 17th century witnessed a remarkable flourishing of artistic and intellectual life in the Dutch Republic, a period now fondly remembered as the Dutch Golden Age. While advancements were made in numerous fields, it is arguably in painting that this era achieved its most enduring and recognizable legacy.

The backdrop to this artistic explosion was the Dutch Revolt (1568-1648), a protracted struggle for independence from Spanish rule. This conflict, though devastating, ultimately forged a new nation, the Republic of the Seven United Netherlands, characterized by its unique political structure, burgeoning economy, and a newfound sense of national identity. This newly won freedom, both political and religious (to a degree), provided fertile ground for artistic innovation. Unlike the heavily religious art of Catholic Europe, the Calvinist-influenced Dutch Republic fostered a more secular approach to art, focusing on everyday life, portraiture, landscapes, and still lifes.

Several key artistic styles defined this period. The early 17th century saw the continuation of Mannerism, characterized by elongated figures, distorted perspectives, and dramatic compositions. However, this style soon gave way to the influence of Italian Baroque, particularly the work of Caravaggio. Dutch artists like Hendrick ter Brugghen, Gerard van Honthorst, and Dirck van Baburen, known as the Utrecht Caravaggisti, traveled to Italy and returned with a taste for dramatic chiaroscuro (the use of strong contrasts between light and dark) and realistic depictions of everyday scenes. This influence is readily apparent in Honthorst's "The Merry Fiddler" (1623), where the dramatic lighting and the lively scene of music-making create a palpable sense of immediacy.

However, the defining style of the Dutch Golden Age was undoubtedly Realism. Dutch artists sought to depict the world around them with meticulous detail and accuracy. This emphasis on realism extended to all genres. In portraiture, artists like Frans Hals captured the fleeting expressions and personalities of their subjects with remarkable skill. His "Banquet of the Officers of the St. George Militia Company in 1616" is a masterpiece of group portraiture, showcasing the camaraderie and individual personalities of the militiamen. Hals' loose brushwork and dynamic compositions breathed life into his subjects, setting him apart from his contemporaries.

Landscape painting also reached new heights of realism and sophistication. Artists like Jan van Goyen, Salomon van Ruysdael, and Jacob van Ruisdael captured the unique Dutch landscape with its flat polders, windmills, and vast skies. Van Goyen's "View of Dordrecht" (1640s) exemplifies this style, with its muted palette and atmospheric perspective creating a sense of vastness and tranquility. Ruisdael, on the other hand, often depicted more dramatic scenes of forests, waterfalls, and stormy skies, showcasing the power of nature. These landscapes were not simply topographical records; they often conveyed symbolic meanings, reflecting the Dutch people's connection to their land and their struggle against the sea.

Still life painting also flourished, with artists like Willem Claesz. Heda, Pieter Claesz., and Rachel Ruysch creating exquisite depictions of everyday objects, from food and flowers to books and musical instruments. These paintings, often brimming with symbolic meaning, were not merely decorative; they also served as reminders of the transience of life and the vanities of the world. Ruysch, one of the few prominent female artists of the era, achieved international acclaim for her meticulously detailed flower paintings, demonstrating the high level of skill and artistry present in this genre.

The art market in the Dutch Republic was unique for its time. Unlike in other parts of Europe, where art was primarily commissioned by the Church or the aristocracy, in the Dutch Republic, a thriving middle class emerged as the primary patrons of art. This created a demand for smaller, more affordable paintings that could decorate the homes of merchants, shopkeepers, and even skilled craftsmen. This democratization of art had a profound impact on the subjects depicted and the way art was produced and consumed. Art became a commodity, traded and sold in open markets and art fairs. This is evidenced by contemporary accounts and inventories, such as those kept by art dealers like Johannes Vermeer's father, which demonstrate the scale and scope of the art market.

This burgeoning art market also led to specialization among artists. Painters focused on specific genres, becoming masters of portraiture, landscape, still life, or genre scenes (depictions of everyday life). This specialization allowed artists to hone their skills and produce high-quality work efficiently. Genre painting, in particular, became immensely popular, with artists like Jan Steen, Gerard ter Borch, and Pieter de Hooch capturing the everyday lives of ordinary people with humor and insight. Steen's "The Merry Family" (1668) is a prime example, depicting a chaotic but lively household scene, offering a glimpse into the social customs and values of the time.

The social and cultural significance of Dutch painting during the Golden Age cannot be overstated. Art was not just a decoration; it played a crucial role in shaping Dutch national identity, reflecting their values, beliefs, and aspirations. The emphasis on realism and the depiction of everyday life reflected the Dutch emphasis on hard work, thrift, and piety. The success of the Dutch Republic, built on trade and commerce, was also reflected in the art of the time, with numerous paintings depicting ships, harbors, and bustling marketplaces.

The Dutch Golden Age of painting was a unique moment in art history. The confluence of political independence, economic prosperity, and a unique social and cultural environment created a fertile ground for artistic innovation. The emphasis on realism, the thriving art market, and the patronage of a broad middle class led to the production of a vast number of paintings, many of which are considered masterpieces today. These works not only provide a window into the lives and values of the Dutch people in the 17th century but also continue to inspire and captivate audiences centuries later. As Simon Schama notes in The Embarrassment of Riches, the Dutch Golden Age was a period of intense self-reflection, and their art was a primary means of expressing and understanding their place in the world. This wealth of artistic output, documented in contemporary sources like inventories, pamphlets discussing art theory, and the paintings themselves, provides a rich tapestry for historians to understand this remarkable period. The legacy of these artists, from Rembrandt's profound explorations of human emotion to Vermeer's serene depictions of domestic life, continues to resonate, cementing the

Dutch Golden Age as a pivotal moment in the history of art.

THE MASTERS (REMBRANDT, VERMEER, HALS)

Within the constellation of brilliant artists that illuminated the Dutch Golden Age, three figures stand out as true luminaries: Rembrandt van Rijn, Johannes Vermeer, and Frans Hals. These masters, each with their distinct style and approach, not only defined the artistic landscape of their time but also left an indelible mark on the history of art.

Rembrandt van Rijn (1606-1669)

Born in Leiden to a miller and a baker's daughter, Rembrandt Harmenszoon van Rijn rose to become arguably the most important artist in Dutch history. His life, marked by both triumph and tragedy, is deeply intertwined with his artistic development. After a brief period at Leiden University, Rembrandt apprenticed with local painters before moving to Amsterdam in the early 1630s. There, he quickly established himself as a sought-after portraitist, attracting wealthy patrons and establishing a successful studio.

Rembrandt's early works, such as "The Anatomy Lesson of Dr. Nicolaes Tulp" (1632), showcase his mastery of composition and his dramatic use of light and shadow, influenced by the Caravaggisti. This painting, a group portrait of surgeons witnessing a public dissection, is a tour-de-force of realism and psychological insight.

However, it was in his later works that Rembrandt truly revealed his genius. He developed a unique style characterized by loose brushwork, rich impasto (thick application of paint), and a profound understanding of human emotion. His portraits, such as the numerous self-portraits he painted throughout his life, are not merely likenesses; they are penetrating studies of character, revealing the inner lives of his subjects.

Rembrandt's most famous work, "The Night Watch" (1642), is a monumental group portrait of a militia company. Despite its misleading nickname (the painting was darkened by centuries of varnish), it is a dynamic and complex composition, showcasing Rembrandt's ability to capture movement and drama. However, this painting also marked a turning point in his career. Its unconventional composition and dramatic lighting were not universally appreciated, and Rembrandt's popularity began to decline.

The later years of Rembrandt's life were marked by personal and financial hardship. He lost his beloved wife Saskia van Uylenburgh in 1642, and he faced increasing financial difficulties, eventually declaring bankruptcy in 1656. Yet, despite these challenges, Rembrandt continued to produce some of his greatest works, including powerful portraits, biblical scenes, and intimate etchings. His late self-portraits, in particular, are deeply moving reflections on aging, loss, and the human condition.

Rembrandt's impact on the history of art is immense. His mastery of light and shadow, his psychological insight, and his innovative techniques influenced generations of artists. His emphasis on individual expression and his exploration of human emotion paved the way for later artistic movements, such as Romanticism and Expressionism.

Johannes Vermeer (1632-1675)

In contrast to Rembrandt's prolific output and dramatic life, Johannes Vermeer led a relatively quiet and uneventful existence in the city of Delft. Little is known about his life, and only around 35 paintings are definitively attributed to him. Yet, despite this limited output, Vermeer is considered one of the greatest painters of the Dutch Golden Age.

Vermeer's paintings are characterized by their serene atmosphere, exquisite use of light, and meticulous attention to detail. His subjects are often quiet domestic scenes, featuring women engaged in everyday activities, such as reading, writing, or pouring milk. His most famous work, "Girl with a Pearl Earring" (c. 1665), is a captivating portrait that has captivated audiences for centuries. The girl's direct gaze and the subtle play of light on her face create a sense of intimacy and mystery.

Vermeer's technique is remarkable for its precision and clarity. He used a technique known as optical mixing, applying thin layers of paint to create luminous colors and subtle gradations of light. He also employed the camera obscura, a device that projects an image onto a surface, to aid in his compositions and perspective. This technique is evident in the precise rendering of light and shadow in his paintings, as well as the accurate depiction of perspective.

Vermeer's paintings were not widely known during his lifetime, and he died in relative obscurity. It was not until the 19th century that his work was rediscovered and recognized for its genius. Today, Vermeer is celebrated for his unique ability to capture the beauty and tranquility of everyday life, elevating the ordinary to the extraordinary.

Frans Hals (c. 1582-1666)

Frans Hals was a master of portraiture, known for his lively and dynamic depictions of people. Born in Antwerp (then part of the Spanish Netherlands), Hals moved to Haarlem as a child and spent most of his life there. He is best known for his group portraits of civic guards and regents, which capture the spirit and camaraderie of these groups.

Hals's style is characterized by his loose brushwork, his ability to capture fleeting expressions, and his sense of spontaneity. His paintings seem to capture a moment in time, as if the subjects have just been caught in conversation or laughter. His most famous work, "Banquet of the Officers of the St. George Militia Company in 1616," is a prime example of his dynamic group portraits. The painting depicts the officers at a banquet, each with their distinct personality and expression.

Hals's ability to capture the vitality of his subjects is also evident in his individual portraits, such as "The Laughing Cavalier" (1624). This portrait, with its infectious smile and lively pose, is one of the most recognizable images of the Dutch Golden Age.

Hals's influence on later artists is significant, particularly on the Impressionists, who admired his loose brushwork and his ability to capture the fleeting effects of light and movement. His paintings continue to inspire and delight viewers with their energy and vitality.

These three masters, Rembrandt, Vermeer, and Hals, each made unique contributions to the Dutch Golden Age of painting. Rembrandt's profound explorations of human emotion, Vermeer's serene depictions of domestic life, and Hals's lively and dynamic portraits cemented their place as giants in the history of art.

Their works continue to inspire and captivate audiences, reminding us of the enduring power of art to illuminate the human experience.

Scientific Discoveries

The Dutch Golden Age was not only a period of artistic flourishing but also a time of significant scientific advancement. The same spirit of inquiry and innovation that drove artistic creation also fueled scientific exploration, leading to groundbreaking discoveries and inventions that transformed our understanding of the world.

The 17th century witnessed a shift in scientific thinking, moving away from reliance on ancient authorities like Aristotle and embracing observation, experimentation, and mathematical reasoning. This "Scientific Revolution," as it is known, was a European phenomenon, but the Dutch Republic played a crucial role, providing a fertile ground for scientific inquiry. The relative freedom of thought and expression in the Republic, compared to other European nations, allowed for the open exchange of ideas and the pursuit of scientific knowledge without undue religious or political interference.

One of the most significant inventions of this period was the microscope. While the principle of magnification had been known for some time, it was in the Dutch Republic that the microscope was developed into a powerful tool for scientific observation. Zacharias Janssen and his son Hans are often credited with the invention of the compound microscope around 1590, although the exact details are somewhat unclear. However, it was Antonie van Leeuwenhoek (1632-1723) who truly revolutionized microscopy.

Leeuwenhoek, a self-taught scientist and lens grinder from Delft, developed incredibly powerful single-lens microscopes that allowed him to observe the microscopic world with unprecedented clarity. He was the first to observe and describe bacteria, protozoa, sperm cells, and blood cells, among other microscopic organisms. His detailed observations, meticulously documented in letters to the Royal Society of London, opened up an entirely new realm of scientific inquiry and laid the foundation for the field of microbiology.

Leeuwenhoek's discoveries had a profound impact on scientific understanding. They challenged existing theories about the nature of life and disease, and they provided new insights into the workings of the human body. His work also had practical applications, contributing to advancements in medicine and public health.

Another key invention of this period was the telescope. While the first telescopes were likely developed in the Netherlands around 1608, with Hans Lipperhey and Jacob Metius both claiming invention, it was Galileo Galilei's astronomical observations with an improved telescope in 1609 that truly revolutionized astronomy. However, Dutch scientists also made significant contributions to the development and use of the telescope.

Christiaan Huygens (1629-1695), a brilliant Dutch mathematician, physicist, and astronomer, made significant improvements to the telescope, including the invention of the Huygens eyepiece, which greatly improved image quality. With his improved telescopes, Huygens made several important astronomical discoveries, including the rings of Saturn and its largest moon, Titan, in 1655. He also made significant contributions to the understanding of light and optics, proposing the wave theory of light.

The invention of the telescope had a profound impact on our understanding of the universe. It confirmed the Copernican heliocentric model of the solar system, which placed the Sun at the center rather than the Earth, and it revealed the vastness and complexity of the cosmos. These discoveries challenged traditional views of the universe and had profound implications for philosophy, religion, and science.

The Dutch Golden Age also saw advancements in other scientific fields, including cartography, medicine, and chemistry. Dutch cartographers, such as Willem Blaeu and Joan Blaeu, produced highly accurate and detailed maps of the world, which were essential for navigation and trade. In medicine, scientists like Reinier de Graaf made important discoveries about the reproductive system.

The relationship between science and society in the Dutch Golden Age was complex and multifaceted. On the one hand, there was a growing interest in science among the general public, fueled by the publication of scientific books and the establishment of public lectures and demonstrations. On the other hand, there was also some resistance to new scientific ideas, particularly those that challenged traditional religious beliefs.

However, the Dutch Republic's unique social and cultural environment, characterized by its commercial spirit, its religious tolerance (to a degree), and its emphasis on education, fostered a climate that was conducive to scientific inquiry. The patronage of wealthy merchants and civic leaders also played a crucial role in supporting scientific research and innovation.

The scientific discoveries of the Dutch Golden Age had a lasting impact on our understanding of the world. The invention of the microscope and the telescope opened up new frontiers of scientific exploration, revealing the microscopic world and the vastness of the cosmos. These discoveries, along with advancements in other scientific fields, transformed our understanding of nature, the human body, and the universe.

The relationship between science and society in the Dutch Golden Age was also significant. The relative freedom of thought and expression in the Republic, combined with the support of a growing scientific community, created a fertile ground for scientific innovation. This period laid the foundation for modern science and continues to inspire scientific inquiry today. This era's scientific achievements, documented in publications like Philosophical Transactions of the Royal Society (to which Leeuwenhoek contributed), scientific treatises, and even artistic depictions of scientific instruments and practices, paint a picture of a society increasingly engaged with empirical observation and the pursuit of knowledge.

CHAPTER 5

TWILIGHT OF THE GOLDEN AGE

The Rampjaar (Disaster Year) of 1672

The Dutch Golden Age, a period of unprecedented prosperity, artistic brilliance, and global influence, seemed destined to endure indefinitely. However, the year 1672, known in Dutch history as the Rampjaar (Disaster Year), shattered this illusion of invincibility. A confluence of political miscalculations, military setbacks, and social unrest brought the Republic to the brink of collapse, marking a turning point in its history and signaling the beginning of the twilight of its Golden Age. This chapter delves into the causes, events, impact, and long-term consequences of this pivotal year.

The seeds of the Rampjaar were sown in the complex political landscape of Europe in the late 17th century. The Dutch Republic, a relatively small nation, had risen to become a major economic and maritime power, challenging the dominance of larger European powers like England and France. This rise inevitably created tensions and rivalries.

One key factor was the ongoing rivalry with England. The two nations had engaged in several naval wars throughout the mid-17th century, vying for control of trade routes and colonial territories. These conflicts, though ultimately ending in Dutch victories, strained the Republic's resources and created a sense of vulnerability. The Second Anglo-Dutch War (1665-1667), for instance, while ending with the Dutch raid on the Medway and a favorable peace treaty, highlighted the potential threat posed by a major naval power.

More significantly, the growing power of France under King Louis XIV posed a direct threat to the Republic's security. Louis XIV, driven by ambitions of territorial expansion and a desire to assert French hegemony in Europe, viewed the Dutch Republic as an obstacle to his plans. He saw the Republic's wealth and Calvinist faith as a challenge to his absolute monarchy and Catholic beliefs.

The political situation within the Republic itself also contributed to its vulnerability. The Republic was a decentralized federation of seven provinces, each with its own government and interests. This decentralized structure, while contributing to its economic dynamism, also made it difficult to coordinate a unified response to external threats. The political landscape was further complicated by the ongoing power struggle between the Stadtholder, traditionally a member of the House of Orange, and the States Party, representing the interests of the wealthy merchant oligarchs.

Johan de Witt, the Grand Pensionary of Holland and the leading figure of the States Party, had successfully maintained peace and prosperity for two decades. He prioritized trade and sought to avoid costly wars, favoring a strong navy over a large standing army. This policy, while beneficial in times of peace, proved disastrous when faced with a land invasion. De Witt and his supporters also deliberately sidelined the House of Orange, fearing their potential to consolidate power and establish a monarchy. This decision, while intended to preserve the republican system, created a deep division within Dutch society, leaving the nation ill-prepared for the crisis to come.

In 1672, Louis XIV launched a massive invasion of the Dutch Republic, supported by England, Münster, and Cologne. This coalition, with its combined military might, overwhelmed the Dutch defenses. The French army, led by skilled generals like Condé and Turenne, quickly overran much of the Republic's eastern territories. The Dutch army, under the command of the inexperienced William III of Orange (the future King William III of England), was ill-prepared and unable to halt the French advance.

The speed and scale of the French invasion shocked the Dutch population. Panic spread throughout the Republic as cities fell to the invaders. The situation was exacerbated by the flooding of the Dutch Water Line, a system of defensive inundations designed to protect the western provinces. While the Water Line ultimately halted the French advance towards Holland's core, it also caused widespread damage and displacement.

The Rampjaar witnessed a surge of popular unrest and anger directed at Johan de Witt and the States Party. The public, desperate for leadership and protection, turned to William of Orange, demanding his appointment as Stadtholder. In August 1672, Johan de Witt and his brother Cornelis were brutally murdered by a mob in The Hague. This horrific event, fueled by misinformation and political propaganda, symbolized the complete breakdown of order and the deep divisions within Dutch society.

William III was subsequently appointed Stadtholder, assuming supreme command of the Dutch forces. He proved to be a capable military leader and a skilled diplomat. He formed alliances with other European powers, including the Holy Roman Empire and Spain, to counter the French threat. The Dutch navy, under the command of Michiel de Ruyter, achieved several crucial naval victories against the combined English and French fleets, preventing a complete naval blockade and maintaining crucial supply lines. De Ruyter's tactical brilliance and strategic thinking are well documented in contemporary accounts and biographies, showcasing his vital role in preventing total defeat.

The combination of the flooded Water Line, Dutch naval victories, and the formation of a European coalition gradually turned the tide of the war. By 1674, the French forces were forced to withdraw from most of the occupied territories. The Treaty of Nijmegen, signed in 1678, formally ended the war, with relatively minor territorial changes for the Republic.

The Rampjaar had a profound impact on Dutch society and politics. The brutal murder of the de Witt brothers left a deep scar on the nation and exposed the fragility of its republican system. The rise of William III as Stadtholder marked a shift towards a more centralized form of government, with the House of Orange gaining significant power. This shift would have long-term consequences for the Dutch Republic, eventually leading to the establishment of a monarchy in the 19th century.

The Rampjaar also had significant economic consequences. The disruption of trade and the costs of the war led to a period of economic decline. While the Republic recovered relatively quickly, it never fully regained its previous level of economic dominance. The war exposed the vulnerability of the Dutch economy to external shocks and marked the beginning of a gradual shift in global economic power towards England.

The Rampjaar also had a significant cultural impact. The sense of national trauma and the experience of near-collapse led to a period of introspection and self-reflection. The events of 1672 were widely documented in pamphlets, broadsides, and other contemporary publications, providing valuable insights into the public mood and the impact of the crisis. The experience also contributed to a growing sense of Dutch national identity, forged in the face of adversity.

In the long term, the Rampjaar marked the beginning of the decline of the Dutch Golden Age. While the Republic continued to be a significant player on the European stage for some time, it never fully recovered its previous level of economic and political dominance. The events of 1672 exposed the limitations of the Republic's political system, its military vulnerability, and the fragility of its economic prosperity. The crisis also demonstrated the importance of strong leadership and national unity in times of adversity. This turning point, well documented in primary sources like the letters of prominent figures such as Constantijn Huygens, as well as in later historical analyses like those by historians like Jonathan Israel, serves as a crucial case study in the dynamics of power, the challenges of maintaining national security, and the cyclical nature of historical fortunes. The Rampjaar stands as a stark reminder that even the most prosperous and powerful nations are not immune to crisis and decline.

The Anglo-Dutch Wars

The 17th century witnessed a series of intense naval conflicts between England and the Dutch Republic, known collectively as the Anglo-Dutch Wars. These wars, fought primarily at sea, were driven by intense commercial rivalry and the struggle for maritime dominance. They significantly impacted both nations, reshaping their naval power, commercial influence, and the overall balance of power in Europe.

The First Anglo-Dutch War (1652-1654)

The First Anglo-Dutch War was rooted in growing commercial competition between the two nations. The English Navigation Act of 1651, which restricted trade with England and its colonies to English ships or ships of the country of origin, was a direct challenge to Dutch dominance in international trade. This act aimed to exclude Dutch shipping from the lucrative trade with English colonies in North America and the Caribbean.

Key events of the war included:

The Battle of Goodwin Sands (1652): An inconclusive opening battle that marked the formal start of the war.

The Battle of Dungeness (1652): A Dutch victory under Admiral Maarten Tromp.

The Battle of the Gabbard (1653): An English victory that inflicted heavy losses on the Dutch fleet.

The Battle of Scheveningen (1653): A decisive English victory that resulted in the death of Admiral Tromp.

The war ended with the Treaty of Westminster in 1654. While the treaty largely reaffirmed the Navigation Act, it also recognized Dutch maritime power. The war demonstrated the strength of both navies and highlighted the importance of naval power in controlling trade routes.

The Second Anglo-Dutch War (1665-1667)

The Second Anglo-Dutch War was also primarily driven by commercial rivalry, particularly in the lucrative trade with Africa and the East Indies. English expansion in these regions, coupled with unresolved issues from the First Anglo-Dutch War, led to renewed tensions.

Key events included:

The Battle of Lowestoft (1665): A significant English victory.

The Four Days' Battle (1666): A hard-fought battle that ended in a Dutch victory.

The Raid on the Medway (1667): A daring Dutch raid led by Admiral Michiel de Ruyter, which saw the Dutch fleet sail up the Medway River and attack the English fleet at anchor, capturing and destroying several ships. This humiliating defeat forced England to negotiate peace.

The war ended with the Treaty of Breda in 1667. This treaty was generally favorable to the Dutch, with England relaxing some of the provisions of the Navigation Act. The Dutch also gained control of Suriname in South America in exchange for New Netherland (present-day New York). The Raid on the

Medway stands as one of the most significant naval victories in Dutch history, demonstrating their naval prowess and forcing England to acknowledge their maritime strength.

The Third Anglo-Dutch War (1672-1674)

The Third Anglo-Dutch War was part of a larger conflict known as the Franco-Dutch War. England, under King Charles II, allied with France against the Dutch Republic. This war was less about direct Anglo-Dutch rivalry and more about England's role in European power politics.

Key events included:

The Battle of Solebay (1672): An inconclusive battle between the combined English and French fleets and the Dutch fleet.

Several other naval engagements: While the English and French initially had the upper hand, the Dutch navy, under De Ruyter's command, managed to prevent a full-scale invasion of the Netherlands.

The war ended with the Treaty of Westminster in 1674, with England making peace with the Dutch Republic.

This treaty largely restored the status quo ante bellum. The Third Anglo-Dutch War was less decisive than the previous two conflicts, but it further demonstrated the resilience of the Dutch navy and its ability to defend its homeland.

Impact of the Anglo-Dutch Wars

The Anglo-Dutch Wars had a profound impact on both nations:

Impact on Dutch Naval Power: The wars initially showcased Dutch naval strength, with admirals like Tromp and De Ruyter achieving significant victories. However, the constant warfare strained Dutch resources and gradually weakened their naval dominance.

Impact on Dutch Commercial Power: The wars disrupted Dutch trade and contributed to a gradual shift in global commercial power towards England. While the Dutch Republic remained a significant commercial power, it never fully regained its previous level of dominance.

Shifting Balance of Power: The Anglo-Dutch Wars marked a gradual shift in the balance of power between England and the Netherlands. While the Dutch Republic remained a major power for some time, England emerged as the dominant maritime and commercial power in the long run.

The Anglo-Dutch Wars were a series of intense conflicts that shaped the course of European history. They demonstrated the importance of naval power in controlling trade routes and influencing global events. These wars also marked a turning point in the relationship between England and the Netherlands, with England gradually eclipsing the Dutch Republic as the dominant maritime and commercial power. The detailed accounts of these battles, found in naval records, contemporary pamphlets, and the biographies of key figures like De Ruyter, offer valuable insights into the strategies, tactics, and consequences of these crucial conflicts.

The Legacy of the Golden Age

The Dutch Golden Age, a period spanning much of the 17th century, represents a remarkable chapter in the history of the Netherlands and the world. This era witnessed an extraordinary flourishing of art, science, culture, and economics, leaving a lasting impact that continues to resonate today.

A Summary of Key Achievements

The Dutch Golden Age was characterized by remarkable achievements across various fields:

Art: As explored in previous chapters, the Golden Age produced some of the greatest painters in history, including Rembrandt van Rijn, Johannes Vermeer, and Frans Hals. Their innovative techniques, masterful use of light and shadow, and profound insights into human nature revolutionized painting and left an indelible mark on art history. The development of distinct genres like landscape, still life, and genre painting, catered to a broad market of art buyers, further distinguishes this period.

Science: This era saw significant scientific advancements, particularly in microscopy and astronomy. Antonie van Leeuwenhoek's pioneering work with the microscope opened up the microscopic world, laying the foundation for microbiology. Christiaan Huygens's contributions to astronomy, optics, and mathematics were equally groundbreaking. The spirit of empirical observation and experimentation, fostered in the relatively tolerant intellectual climate of the Dutch Republic, contributed significantly to the Scientific Revolution.

Culture: The Dutch Golden Age was a period of vibrant cultural activity. Literature, philosophy, and theater flourished. Writers like Joost van den Vondel produced influential plays and poems, while philosophers like Hugo Grotius laid the foundations for modern international law. The relative freedom of the press in the Republic allowed for the widespread dissemination of ideas, contributing to a lively public discourse.

Economics: The Dutch Republic became a leading economic power in the 17th century, driven by its dominance in international trade, shipping, and finance. The establishment of the Dutch East India

Company (VOC) and the Dutch West India Company (WIC) facilitated global trade and colonial expansion. Amsterdam became a major financial center, with the establishment of the Amsterdam Stock Exchange and the Bank of Amsterdam. This economic prowess was inextricably linked to their naval dominance, which secured trade routes and protected their commercial interests.

Lasting Impact on the Netherlands and the World

The legacy of the Dutch Golden Age is multifaceted and far-reaching:

National Identity: The Golden Age played a crucial role in shaping Dutch national identity. The achievements of this era became a source of national pride and a symbol of Dutch resilience, ingenuity, and cultural achievement. The memory of the struggle for independence from Spain, culminating in the establishment of the Republic, and the subsequent period of prosperity and cultural flourishing, solidified a sense of national unity and purpose.

Artistic Influence: The Dutch Masters of the Golden Age had a profound impact on the development of

Western art. Their techniques, styles, and subject matter influenced generations of artists, from the Impressionists to modern painters. The emphasis on realism, the exploration of light and shadow, and the focus on everyday life continue to be relevant in contemporary art.

Scientific Legacy: The scientific discoveries of the Golden Age, particularly in microscopy and astronomy, had a transformative impact on scientific understanding. Leeuwenhoek's work laid the foundation for microbiology, while Huygens's contributions to optics and astronomy advanced our understanding of the universe. The emphasis on empirical observation and experimentation, championed by Dutch scientists, continues to be a cornerstone of scientific methodology.

Economic and Financial Systems: The Dutch Republic's innovative economic and financial institutions, such as the VOC, the Amsterdam Stock Exchange, and the Bank of Amsterdam, had a lasting impact on the development of modern capitalism. The VOC's pioneering use of joint-stock companies and its vast global trading network set a precedent for future multinational corporations. The Amsterdam Stock Exchange established a model for modern stock exchanges, while the Bank of Amsterdam played a crucial role in the development of modern banking practices.

Legal and Philosophical Thought: Hugo Grotius's work on international law, particularly his book De Jure Belli ac Pacis (On the Law of War and Peace), laid the foundations for modern international legal principles. His ideas on natural law and the rights of nations continue to be influential in international relations and legal theory. The relative freedom of thought and expression in the Dutch Republic also contributed to the development of Enlightenment ideas, which would have a profound impact on European and global history.

Remembering and Interpreting the Golden Age Today

The Dutch Golden Age continues to be a subject of fascination and study today. It is remembered and interpreted in various ways:

National Commemoration: The Golden Age is celebrated in the Netherlands as a period of national greatness. Museums, historical sites, and cultural events commemorate the achievements of this era. The Rijksmuseum in Amsterdam, for instance, houses a vast collection of Golden Age art, attracting millions of visitors each year.

Historical Scholarship: Historians continue to research and analyze the Golden Age, exploring its various aspects and offering new interpretations. Recent scholarship has focused on topics such as the social and economic inequalities of the period, the role of women in Golden Age society, and the impact of Dutch colonialism.

Cultural Representation: The Golden Age is also represented in popular culture, through films, novels, and other forms of media. These representations often portray the Golden Age as a time of adventure, discovery, and artistic brilliance, but they also sometimes address the darker aspects of the period, such as slavery and colonial exploitation.

Debates and Reinterpretations: While the Golden Age is often celebrated as a period of national triumph, there are also ongoing debates about its legacy. Some historians and commentators have criticized the focus on the positive aspects of the era, arguing that it overlooks the negative consequences of Dutch colonialism and the exploitation of enslaved people. This re-evaluation of the Golden Age is part of a broader trend of reassessing historical narratives and acknowledging the complexities of the past.

The interpretation of the Golden Age has evolved over time. In the past, it was often presented as a straightforward narrative of national triumph. However, contemporary interpretations are more nuanced, acknowledging both the achievements and the complexities of this period. There is a growing recognition of the need to address the darker aspects of the Golden Age, such as the role of slavery in the Dutch economy and the impact of Dutch colonialism on other parts of the world.

The legacy of the Dutch Golden Age is complex and multifaceted. It represents a period of remarkable achievements in art, science, culture, and economics, which have had a lasting impact on the Netherlands and the world. However, it is also important to acknowledge the darker aspects of this era and to engage with the ongoing debates about its legacy. By understanding the complexities of the past, we can gain a deeper understanding of the present and work towards a more just and equitable future. The numerous primary sources available, ranging from VOC records to personal letters and diaries, combined with ongoing scholarly research, ensure that the Dutch Golden Age continues to be a rich and dynamic field of study, offering valuable insights into the forces that shape societies and the enduring impact of historical events.

Conclusion

The Dutch Golden Age, as we've explored, was a period of extraordinary dynamism and achievement. From the brushstrokes of Rembrandt and Vermeer to the scientific breakthroughs of Leeuwenhoek and Huygens, this era left an indelible mark on art, science, culture, and global commerce. It was a time of both triumph and turmoil, a complex tapestry woven with threads of innovation, prosperity, conflict, and societal change. The legacy of this period continues to shape the Netherlands and resonates across the world. We hope this journey through the Golden Age has provided you with a deeper understanding of this fascinating period in history. If you enjoyed this exploration and found it informative, we would be incredibly grateful if you would consider leaving a positive review and rating on Amazon. Your feedback helps other readers discover this captivating era and supports our continued efforts to bring history to life.